Gifts of the Season: 100 Christmas Poems

Dwight Edmond

Published by Bright Minds Books, 2024.

While every precaution has been taken in the preparation of this book, the publisher assumes no responsibility for errors or omissions, or for damages resulting from the use of the information contained herein.

GIFTS OF THE SEASON: 100 CHRISTMAS POEMS

First edition. November 25, 2024.

Copyright © 2024 Dwight Edmond.

ISBN: 979-8230328483

Written by Dwight Edmond.

Table of Contents

Description

Discover the magic of Christmas through *Gifts of the Season: A Collection of Christmas Poems*.

This heartwarming anthology features 100 enchanting poems that celebrate the spirit of giving, the joy of kindness, and the beauty of holiday surprises. Each six-stanza poem captures the essence of Christmas, weaving tales of love, warmth, and togetherness.

Perfect for cozy nights by the fire or as a thoughtful gift, this collection invites readers of all ages to experience the wonder of the season. Let these verses transport you to a world where Christmas lights shine bright and hearts are forever touched.

Dedication

To all who cherish the magic of Christmas,
This collection is dedicated to you.
May its verses bring warmth to your hearth,
Joy to your heart, and peace to your soul.
And to my family and friends,
Your love and support make every season bright.
Thank you for filling my life with endless cheer.

Preface

Christmas is more than a day—it's a feeling, a cherished time when we gather close to those we love and celebrate the beauty of giving and connection. *Gifts of the Season* was born out of my desire to capture that magic in verse, to reflect on the small moments that make Christmas extraordinary: the twinkle of lights, the laughter of children, and the quiet peace of a snowy night.

This collection brings together 100 poems, each written to inspire joy and reflection. Whether you're revisiting beloved traditions or creating new ones, I hope these poems become part of your holiday journey.

1. The First Gift of Christmas

The snowflakes drift, a gentle song,
The world aglow where hearts belong.
A humble gift, a tender light,
Illuminates this sacred night.
With open hands, we give and share,
The magic lingers in the air.
A spark of joy, a fleeting flame,
In every heart, it stakes its claim.
The greatest gift, so pure, divine,
A love that weaves through space and time.
In giving, we receive anew,
A bond of grace between me and you.
The tree adorned with ribbons bright,
A beacon in the quiet night.
Each gift beneath tells stories told,
Of love and care worth more than gold.
Let every heart, both near and far,
Shine brightly like a Christmas star.
For in the giving, we arise,
To see the world through kinder eyes.
So take this gift, and pass it on,
The light of love will never be gone.
For Christmas lives where giving grows,
A timeless truth that every heart knows.

2. The Sound of Christmas Bells

The bells ring out on frosted air,
A melody beyond compare.
They echo through the quiet streets,
With every chime, a heart it greets.
Their golden tones, both soft and clear,
Bring warmth and cheer to those who hear.
They call to all, both young and old,
A timeless tale in tones retold.
These bells sing of a gift divine,
Of peace and love, a holy sign.
They whisper hope and joy anew,
To every soul, both me and you.
Each chime a wish, each toll a prayer,
For kindness spreading everywhere.
They weave a song of love and grace,
That lights the heart, no time can erase.
So listen close, as bells resound,
Their echoes filling all around.
For Christmas lives in every note,
A joyful hymn the angels wrote.

3. Under the Christmas Tree

Beneath the boughs of evergreen,
A world of wonder can be seen.
Bright paper wraps and ribbons twirl,
A treasure trove for every girl.
Each gift bestowed with thought and care,
A symbol of the love we share.
But more than what is wrapped so tight,
It's joy that makes this season bright.
The tree stands tall, its branches gleam,
With ornaments that catch the beam.
A star atop, it seems to say,
"Rejoice! For this is Christmas Day!"
But gifts are more than things we hold,
They're smiles, and laughs, and hearts of gold.
The gift of love, the gift of cheer,
Are treasures that we hold all year.
So gather round and take your place,
Let love and laughter fill this space.
For under the tree, it's plain to see,
The greatest gift is family.
With every present, every bow,
A deeper truth begins to show:
It's not the gifts but love we find,
That makes this season truly kind.

4. A Candle in the Window

A candle glows in frosty night,
Its flicker casts a gentle light.
A beacon for the ones who roam,
To guide them to their Christmas home.
Its golden flame, so soft, so bright,
Holds warmth against the chilling night.
It whispers peace, it sings of rest,
For weary hearts to feel their best.
Each flicker tells a tale of old,
Of shepherds watching flocks in cold.
Of wise men traveling far and near,
To find the Savior they revere.
The candle stands, a symbol true,
Of hope for all, both me and you.
It lights the path, it shows the way,
To joy and love this Christmas Day.
So let it shine upon your sill,
A flame that warms, a light that fills.
For every heart needs such a glow,
A candle's warmth through ice and snow.
And as it burns through darkest skies,
It teaches us where beauty lies.
In kindness shared, in love's embrace,
We find the light of Christmas grace.

5. A Visit from Saint Nicholas

Upon the roof, a clatter rings,
The sound of hoofbeats swiftly brings.
A sleigh arrives in frosty flight,
With gifts to share this wondrous night.
Old Saint Nick, with sack in hand,
Brings joy and cheer across the land.
Through chimneys wide, through chimneys small,
He delivers magic to them all.
His laugh, a jolly, merry sound,
Brings happiness to all around.
With every gift, his heart bestows,
A joy that only Christmas knows.
The stockings hung by fire's glow,
Are filled with treasures, row by row.
But more than toys or sweets inside,
It's love and warmth that truly abide.
With sleigh bells jingling in the air,
He spreads his cheer beyond compare.
Then up he goes, into the sky,
With a hearty laugh and a fond goodbye.
"To all," he shouts, "a good night's rest,
May Christmas fill your hearts with zest!"
And with a wink, he disappears,
But leaves behind the season's cheers.

6. The Spirit of Giving

The spirit of giving fills the air,
It wraps us in its tender care.
A simple act, a helping hand,
Spreads joy across this snowy land.
From ringing bells to carols sung,
In every heart, the joy is sprung.
For Christmas thrives in deeds so kind,
In every gift, our love we find.
A coat for one who feels the cold,
A friendly call for those grown old.
A plate of food, a warm embrace,
Brings Christmas cheer to every place.
No gift too small, no act too slight,
Can dim the glow of Christmas light.
For in these deeds, we come to see,
The heart of what this day should be.
So as we gather, one and all,
Remember those who feel so small.
Let giving be the gift we share,
To show the world how much we care.
For in the end, it's love we bring,
That makes the Christmas spirit sing.
With every kindness, let us say,
"We keep the spirit every day."

7. The Magic of Christmas Eve

The quiet hush of Christmas Eve,
A night of wonders we believe.
The world prepares for joy to start,
As dreams take root in every heart.
The stars above in silence gleam,
They weave a gentle, peaceful dream.
A night where hope and love combine,
To mark the birth of the divine.
The stockings hung with care and pride,
Await the gifts that lay inside.
But more than toys, it's love they bring,
A melody the heart will sing.
The magic swirls in candlelight,
It dances softly through the night.
It whispers truths we hold so dear,
Of kindness shared this time of year.
For Christmas Eve is more than time,
It's when our spirits truly shine.
With every hug, with every cheer,
We weave the joy that draws us near.
So cherish every precious sound,
Of laughter, love, and peace profound.
For in this night, our hearts will weave,
The magic found on Christmas Eve.

8. The Gift of a Smile

A smile can light the darkest night,
It spreads like fire, warm and bright.
No gift can match its gentle charm,
It holds the power to disarm.
A smile is free, yet priceless still,
It bends the strongest, stubborn will.
It bridges gaps, it mends the heart,
It brings us close, though miles apart.
This season bright, let smiles abound,
In every face, let joy be found.
For even strangers passing by,
Can find a friend in a smiling eye.
The greatest gift, so soft, so sweet,
Requires no bow, needs no receipt.
It's shared with love, it's passed along,
It lifts the weak, it makes us strong.
So give this gift to all you meet,
A smile as bright as Christmas sweet.
For in its warmth, both young and old,
Find treasures worth far more than gold.
And as it spreads from face to face,
It fills the world with love and grace.
This simple act, both pure and true,
Can make the season shine anew.

9. The Christmas Feast

The table set, the candles glow,
A feast prepared with love to show.
The turkey roasts, the spices blend,
A meal where hearts and spirits mend.
The family gathers, hand in hand,
To share the gifts of this great land.
With every dish, a story told,
Of memories cherished, new and old.
The laughter rings, the toasts are made,
As bonds of love will not degrade.
Together here, we celebrate,
With joy and thanks, our hearts elate.
The Christmas feast, a time to share,
Not just the food, but love and care.
For every plate, both full and small,
Holds more than meals—it feeds us all.
And as we dine, we pause to see,
The joy in simple unity.
The feast reminds us, year by year,
The greatest gift is being near.
So raise a glass, and join the cheer,
For Christmas magic lingers here.
In every bite, in every laugh,
We find the love that lights our path.

10. The Snowman's Cheer

The snow falls soft on Christmas morn,
A world of white is freshly born.
And in the yard, with laugh and play,
A snowman stands to greet the day.
With coal for eyes and scarf of red,
A sturdy hat upon his head.
He stands so proud, with stick arms wide,
A jolly figure, full of pride.
The children dance around his form,
Their laughter bright, their hearts so warm.
For in his smile, they see the cheer,
That only comes this time of year.
Though winter winds may howl and blow,
Our snowman stands through ice and snow.
A symbol of the joys we make,
With every flake, a new memory's stake.
And when the sun begins to rise,
He melts but leaves a sweet surprise.
For in their hearts, his joy will stay,
To light their world on Christmas Day.
So let him stand, our frosty friend,
A cheerful sign that love won't end.
For every snowman, near or far,
Holds Christmas magic, just like a star.

11. The Joy of Secret Surprises

A quiet box, a hidden treat,
A secret waiting to complete.
The thrill of giving, kept unseen,
Adds magic to the Christmas scene.
With stealthy steps, the gifts are placed,
A joyful smile hides every trace.
The giver waits, with bated breath,
For moments filled with joy and mirth.
The wrapping tears, the ribbon flies,
And wonder fills the wide-eyed skies.
A gift so simple, yet so grand,
Delivered by a loving hand.
But more than what the gift contains,
It's joy that courses through the veins.
A secret shared, a bond made tight,
Illuminates the darkest night.
For Christmas holds such sweet surprise,
It lights the world before our eyes.
So let us cherish every glance,
And take this chance to share, to dance.
The joy of giving, plain and true,
Is the gift that binds both me and you.
For in each heart, a treasure lies,
Unlocked by love, to our surprise.

12. The Joy of Giving

The joy of giving, pure and sweet,
Makes Christmas truly feel complete.
A thoughtful gift, a helping hand,
Spreads kindness all across the land.
No matter if the gift is small,
It's love that matters most of all.
For when we give, our hearts expand,
And joy is shared across the land.
A coat, a toy, a heartfelt note,
Are treasures more than gold or vote.
They carry warmth, they carry cheer,
To brighten lives throughout the year.
The act of giving sparks a flame,
A simple deed that earns no fame.
Yet in its glow, both giver and friend,
Find bonds of love that never end.
So as we wrap each ribbon tight,
Let's give with hearts both pure and light.
For in our giving, joy will grow,
A gift that all the world will know.
This joy will last through winter's chill,
And bloom like spring on every hill.
For Christmas joy, when shared with care,
Can fill the world, both far and near.

13. Christmas Morning Magic

The morning breaks with soft delight,
A world transformed in snowy white.
The house awakes, the laughter flows,
As Christmas morning joy bestows.
The children race with eager eyes,
To see what gifts beneath them lie.
Each bow untied, each paper torn,
Reveals surprises, joy reborn.
But more than toys, it's love they find,
In every gift, so gently signed.
For Christmas morning's magic lives,
In every act that love forgives.
The stockings bulge with treats and cheer,
A testament to those held dear.
And as the morning stretches on,
The bond of family grows strong.
So let us pause, in midst of play,
To cherish moments of the day.
For Christmas morning comes and goes,
But love remains, and ever grows.
With every hug, with every laugh,
We walk together, light our path.
For Christmas magic, soft and sweet,
Is found where love and family meet.

14. A Christmas Wish

Upon a star so high and bright,
I cast a wish this Christmas night.
A simple hope, a whispered prayer,
For love and peace to fill the air.
May kindness bloom in every heart,
And bring us close, though far apart.
May every home, both large and small,
Feel Christmas joy for one and all.
Let no one face the night alone,
But find in others, hearts of stone.
Let giving hands and caring smiles,
Bridge distances and span the miles.
For every wish sent through the skies,
Is answered where true love abides.
And Christmas teaches, year by year,
That hope and joy can conquer fear.
So make a wish, and let it fly,
On wings of love, through frosty sky.
And may it find, where e'er it lands,
A world united, holding hands.
Together, we can make it true,
This Christmas wish for me and you.
For in our hearts, the answer lies,
A love that lifts, a hope that flies.

15. The Choir's Song

The choir sings a song of old,
A tale of love and joy retold.
Their voices rise in harmony,
A hymn of peace for all to see.
The carols echo through the night,
Their melodies, a soft delight.
They tell of shepherds, stars, and kings,
Of angels bright with golden wings.
Each note they sing, so pure, so true,
Carries a message old yet new.
A promise made in ages past,
Of love and hope that always last.
The choir's song, a gentle breeze,
Brings warmth and calm to hearts at ease.
It lifts the soul, it soothes the mind,
And leaves the woes of life behind.
So let us join their joyful sound,
And let our hearts in love be bound.
For in their song, the truth is clear,
That Christmas lives in hearts sincere.
Together, let our voices blend,
A chorus that will never end.
For Christmas carols, sung with glee,
Spread joy and peace eternally.

16. The Warmth of a Christmas Fire

The fire glows, its embers bright,
A beacon on this winter night.
It crackles soft, it hums a tune,
That warms the heart beneath the moon.
Around the hearth, we gather near,
To share in love and Christmas cheer.
The stories told, the laughter shared,
Are treasures far beyond compared.
The flicker dances on each face,
Illuminating love's embrace.
It whispers warmth, it sings of peace,
A moment where all troubles cease.
The fire burns, yet more than flame,
It holds a power none can name.
A symbol of the love we share,
A light that brightens coldest air.
So as we sit, with hearts alight,
Let's cherish this, a wondrous night.
For in this warmth, both old and new,
We find the spirit, pure and true.
The Christmas fire, a sacred glow,
Reminds us of the love we sow.
And as it burns, it brings us near,
To all we hold most dear this year.

17. The Joy of Christmas Lights

The Christmas lights, they twinkle bright,
A sparkling wonder through the night.
They line the streets, they deck the trees,
A joyful sight for all to see.
Each bulb a glow of festive cheer,
A symbol of the love we bear.
They guide us home through frosty air,
A shining path of love and care.
The reds, the greens, the golden hues,
Bring Christmas magic, pure and true.
They light the way for those who stray,
To find the joy of Christmas Day.
The world transformed by twinkling light,
Is wrapped in warmth on winter nights.
And as they gleam, they softly say,
That love will guide us on our way.
So let them shine, these tiny stars,
They link our hearts, no matter how far.
For Christmas lights, so small, so bright,
Remind us of love's endless light.
With every glow, with every gleam,
They turn the night to joyful dream.
For Christmas magic, shining clear,
Is found in every light, my dear.

18. The Christmas Star

The Christmas star shines high above,
A guiding light of endless love.
It points the way through night so deep,
To where our hearts their promise keep.
Its glow reminds of long ago,
When wise men traveled through the snow.
They followed bright its steady gleam,
To find the child of whom we dream.
This star, a beacon in the sky,
Brings hope to all who wonder why.
It whispers soft of peace and grace,
And lights the path to love's embrace.
No matter where our journeys end,
Its glow will guide and softly send.
A message pure, both strong and clear,
That Christmas joy is always near.
So when you see it shining bright,
Remember love's eternal light.
For in its beams, both near and far,
We find our home, our Christmas star.
Let hearts lift high, let spirits soar,
As Christmas light reveals once more,
That even through the darkest night,
There shines a love forever bright.

19. The Carolers' Delight

Through snowy streets, the carolers go,
Their voices rise in evening glow.
They sing of joy, they sing of peace,
Their harmonies bring sweet release.
From door to door, their music spreads,
A soothing balm for weary heads.
The songs of old, the tunes so grand,
Unite the hearts across the land.
Each note they sing, a tale unfolds,
Of shepherds brave and gifts of gold.
Of angel choirs and skies so bright,
Proclaiming love on silent night.
The carolers bring more than cheer,
They spread the warmth of Christmas near.
For in their songs, the heart can see,
A world at peace, in harmony.
So open wide your door tonight,
And let their songs bring pure delight.
For Christmas carols, sung with heart,
Are gifts of love, a work of art.
And as their voices fade away,
Their echoes in your soul will stay.
For carols sung on frosty nights,
Keep Christmas joy in endless sights.

20. The Christmas Train

The Christmas train rolls down the track,
With dreams and treasures in its stack.
It winds through towns and snowy hills,
A wonderland that warms and thrills.
Its whistle blows a cheerful tune,
Beneath the stars and silver moon.
Each car is filled with gifts and cheer,
To spread the joy of Christmas near.
The children wave as it goes by,
With wide-eyed wonder, hearts on high.
They dream of journeys yet to take,
Of Christmas magic wide awake.
The train connects both far and near,
It brings the gift of love sincere.
For every stop and every start,
It carries joy to every heart.
So board the train, let's ride along,
Through lands of laughter, lights, and song.
For Christmas lives on every track,
With every mile, it gives us back.
And when the journey meets its end,
We'll find ourselves with family, friends.
For Christmas train, both fast and slow,
Brings joy and love where'er we go.

21. The Christmas Cookie

The kitchen fills with scents so sweet,
Of sugar, spice, and doughy treat.
The cookies bake in oven warm,
A holiday in every form.
With icing swirls and sprinkles bright,
They bring a joy, a sheer delight.
A simple gift, both small and true,
Each bite contains a world anew.
The children gather, hands at work,
To spread the cheer with every smirk.
They share their treats with love and pride,
A sweetness that will not subside.
The joy of cookies, soft and round,
Is in the love that does abound.
For every batch, both fresh and warm,
Is made with care in every form.
So break a cookie, share a bite,
And let its warmth make spirits light.
For in its taste, we come to know,
The simple joys that Christmas shows.
Together round the table's glow,
We share the love that cookies sow.
And with each bite, our hearts will sing,
Of Christmas cheer and all it brings.

22. The Sleigh Ride

The sleigh bells ring in frosty air,
A joyful sound beyond compare.
Through snowy fields, the sleigh does glide,
With love and laughter side by side.
The horses trot, their manes aglow,
Their steps crunch softly in the snow.
Beneath the blankets, snug and tight,
We ride through magic's gentle light.
The stars above, the moon so near,
Enhance the Christmas atmosphere.
Each jingle-jangle brings delight,
On this serene and peaceful night.
The ride is short, yet feels so grand,
A cherished journey, hand in hand.
For in the sleigh, we find our peace,
A moment where all worries cease.
So let us ride through winter's gleam,
And hold on tight to Christmas dream.
For in this sleigh, with bells so clear,
We find the joy of Yuletide cheer.
With every laugh and every song,
The Christmas sleigh will speed along.
And leave behind a trail of glee,
A lasting mark on memory.

23. The Silent Gift

A silent gift, no words to speak,
Yet carries strength when hearts are weak.
A simple deed, a thoughtful care,
Can lift the soul from dark despair.
A door held wide, a coat to spare,
A moment shown of love's repair.
For in the silence, kindness blooms,
And clears away the darkest glooms.
The gift of time, a hand held tight,
Transforms the coldest winter night.
It whispers love in quiet ways,
A silent song that always stays.
No ribbon wrapped, no card required,
Just love that burns like hearts inspired.
The silent gift, though often small,
Becomes the greatest gift of all.
So give this gift, both pure and true,
To those in need, both old and new.
For Christmas speaks, in acts not said,
A silent love that's widely spread.
And as you give, you'll find it's clear,
This quiet gift brings Christmas near.
For in its stillness, hearts will know,
The deepest love that life bestows.

24. The Christmas Market

The market glows with festive light,
A bustling scene of pure delight.
With every stall, a story's told,
Of treasures new and trinkets old.
The scents of cinnamon and pine,
Entwine with laughter, sweet and fine.
The chatter hums, the joy abounds,
As Christmas magic wraps around.
From hand-knit scarves to toys and treats,
Each corner holds a special feat.
A gift for all, both young and old,
Is waiting there in hues of gold.
The carolers sing their joyful tune,
Beneath the stars and winter moon.
Their melodies weave through the air,
A timeless song for all to share.
The market stands, a beacon bright,
A hub of cheer on winter nights.
It brings together hearts and hands,
In love that every soul understands.
So wander through this joyful place,
And see the wonder on each face.
For Christmas lives in sights and sounds,
In every market's merry grounds.

25. The Christmas Wreath

A wreath adorned with green and red,
Hangs proudly on the door ahead.
Its circle shape, unbroken, true,
Speaks of the love that binds me and you.
With holly sprigs and berries bright,
It welcomes all on Christmas night.
A symbol of the season's cheer,
That brings us joy year after year.
Each needle points to love's embrace,
A sign of warmth in winter's face.
It whispers softly, "Come inside,
Where love and laughter both reside."
The wreath does more than decorate,
It draws us near, it celebrates.
For in its boughs, a promise laid,
Of peace and joy, of love displayed.
So hang your wreath with gentle care,
Let its bright spirit fill the air.
For Christmas wreaths, so bold and true,
Bring hearts together, me and you.
And every year, its meaning grows,
A timeless truth that Christmas shows.
For love, like wreaths, will never end,
It circles round to hearts, my friend.

26. The Chimney's Tale

The chimney stands, both tall and wide,
A secret path for Santa's ride.
It waits in stillness, calm and cool,
A bridge between the house and Yule.
Through sooty flue, he makes his way,
On Christmas Eve, without delay.
With sack in tow and boots so black,
He carries cheer upon his back.
The stockings hung along the side,
Will soon with treasures be supplied.
And as he works, his hearty laugh,
Echoes soft through chimney's shaft.
The chimney tells of years gone by,
Of countless nights and starry skies.
Each brick recalls the joy and cheer,
That Santa brings, year after year.
And when he's done, he gives a wink,
Then vanishes before we blink.
The chimney cools, but keeps inside,
The magic of that Yuletide ride.
So as you rest on Christmas night,
Think of the chimney's secret flight.
For in its depths, the stories stay,
Of love and gifts on Christmas Day.

27. The Christmas Stockings

The stockings hang with gentle care,
Their emptiness a hopeful prayer.
For soon they'll brim with treasures sweet,
A Christmas morning's joyful treat.
Each stocking tells a tale of old,
Of wishes made, of dreams retold.
From candies bright to little toys,
They hold the hopes of girls and boys.
The fireplace hums a quiet song,
As stockings wait the whole night long.
They're symbols of the love we give,
Of joy and cheer through lives we live.
Come morning light, with eyes aglow,
The children rush to see the show.
Each stocking spills its merry hoard,
A feast of gifts the night has stored.
But more than what they hold inside,
It's love and thought that truly guide.
For stockings, though they may seem small,
Reflect the care we give to all.
So hang them high, with hearts sincere,
Let Christmas fill the atmosphere.
For every stocking, plain or grand,
Is touched by love's unending hand.

28. The Gift of Time

The greatest gift we give is time,
A treasure worth more than a dime.
It costs no gold, it bears no bow,
Yet in its warmth, true love will show.
A moment shared, a hand held tight,
Can turn the dark to shining light.
For in those hours spent together,
We weave a bond that lasts forever.
No toy or trinket could replace,
The joy of time in love's embrace.
A game, a laugh, a story told,
Are memories more dear than gold.
So let us give this precious gift,
And see how hearts begin to lift.
For time, once given, can't be sold,
But lingers on as we grow old.
At Christmas, let this truth be known,
That time with loved ones brightly shown,
Is more than gifts beneath the tree,
It's love in its purest decree.
And as the years drift gently by,
These moments shine, they never die.
For time well spent, with hearts aligned,
Is the greatest gift we'll ever find.

29. The Whisper of Winter

Winter whispers through the trees,
Its breath a soft and icy breeze.
It lays a blanket, pure and white,
Transforming all with frosted light.
The world grows still, a quiet peace,
As nature finds a sweet release.
And in this calm, the season brings,
The joy of all that Christmas sings.
The snowflakes dance, a gentle show,
They sparkle bright where moonbeams glow.
Each flake unique, each one a part,
Of winter's art that warms the heart.
The world, though cold, feels warm inside,
As love and cheer through homes abide.
For winter's chill, with all its might,
Cannot outshine the Christmas light.
So let the winter winds declare,
A season full of love and care.
For in its whisper, soft and true,
Is Christmas joy for me and you.
The frost may nip, the cold may bite,
But hearts stay warm on Christmas night.
For winter's whisper softly sings,
Of love and peace that Christmas brings.

30. The Christmas Blanket

A blanket warm, so soft and fine,
Wraps loved ones close as stars align.
Its woven threads of red and green,
Embrace the joy of Christmas scene.
By fireside glow, it finds its place,
A sheltering warmth, a snug embrace.
Through winter's chill, it holds us near,
A symbol of love's atmosphere.
Each stitch, a story, tightly bound,
Of laughter shared and love profound.
It covers all with gentle care,
A comfort rich beyond compare.
The Christmas blanket speaks of peace,
Of love that grants a sweet release.
It shields from cold, both heart and hand,
A warmth that all can understand.
So drape it round, and feel its grace,
A treasure in this special space.
For every home, both far and near,
Deserves such warmth, this time of year.
And long after the snow has gone,
The blanket's love will linger on.
A gift of warmth, a gift of cheer,
To carry through the coming year.

31. The Gift Beneath the Snow

Beneath the snow, so pure and white,
There lies a gift of great delight.
The earth, though sleeping, gently keeps,
A hidden world in winter's sleep.
The frost may glitter, cold and bright,
But underneath, new life takes flight.
It waits in stillness, safe and sound,
Till springtime calls it from the ground.
This secret gift, though out of view,
Reminds us all of life anew.
For even in the darkest days,
Hope stirs within in quiet ways.
At Christmas time, we too can find,
A gift of peace within the mind.
It's not in boxes, bows, or lights,
But deep within, where hope ignites.
So as the snow lies still and deep,
Know that the earth is not asleep.
It cradles life, it holds its grace,
A hidden gift in nature's embrace.
And when the thaw begins to show,
The gift beneath will start to grow.
A sign that love and life endure,
A Christmas gift, both strong and pure.

32. The Reindeer's Flight

Through starry skies, the reindeer fly,
With Santa's sleigh, they soar on high.
Their hooves a blur, their antlers gleam,
They carry forth the Christmas dream.
From house to house, from town to town,
They never let the sleigh touch down.
Their task is grand, their pace is swift,
To spread the joy of every gift.
Each reindeer knows their special role,
Together pulling toward one goal.
Through icy winds and snowy air,
They journey on with strength and care.
The leader lights their way so bright,
A beacon through the darkest night.
His nose aglow, a guiding spark,
To steer the sleigh through cold and dark.
The reindeer's flight, a wondrous sight,
Brings hope and cheer on Christmas night.
For in their speed and in their grace,
They carry love to every place.
So as you sleep on Christmas Eve,
Know that they're near, and just believe.
For reindeer flying through the skies,
Are Christmas magic in disguise.

33. The Christmas Quilt

The Christmas quilt, a patchwork bold,
Tells stories new and stories old.
Each square a piece of love and care,
A tapestry beyond compare.
The reds and greens, the golden threads,
Adorn the quilt upon our beds.
It wraps us close on chilly nights,
A shield against the frosted lights.
Each patch is sewn with hands that know,
The warmth of love that quilts bestow.
A grandmother's touch, a mother's hand,
Creates a piece that understands.
This quilt is more than fabric stitched,
It's love and memories enriched.
It holds the laughter, tears, and cheer,
Of every Christmas through the years.
So spread it wide and snuggle tight,
Beneath its warmth on Christmas night.
For every thread and every seam,
Carries the love of Christmas dream.
And when the season's passed once more,
The quilt remains, a treasure's store.
A timeless gift that we'll recall,
The Christmas quilt that wraps us all.

34. A Letter to Santa

A letter written, plain and neat,
With wishes bold and dreams so sweet.
It travels far on winter breeze,
To reach old Santa 'cross the seas.
Each word a hope, each line a plea,
For joy and gifts beneath the tree.
But more than toys, the letter shows,
A heart that loves, a heart that grows.
The elves will read with careful eye,
Each wish beneath the snowy sky.
They'll craft and wrap with cheerful speed,
To meet each child's heartfelt need.
But Santa knows, beyond the list,
It's love and care that can't be missed.
He sends his blessings far and wide,
With every sleigh ride, every stride.
So write your letters, young and old,
With dreams and hopes that won't grow cold.
For Santa reads them, one by one,
And spreads the joy when Christmas comes.
And though the gifts may come and go,
The love within will always show.
For letters sent on Christmas Eve,
Bring magic back to those who believe.

35. The Christmas Garland

The garland drapes in flowing green,
A festive touch to every scene.
It winds around the banister,
And frames the hearth with fragrant fir.
With pinecones nestled, ribbons tied,
It brings the forest deep inside.
A rustic charm, a woodland grace,
Transforms the home to a cozy space.
The garland tells of ancient woods,
Of winter's peace and nature's goods.
Its evergreen, a lasting sign,
Of life and love through wintertime.
Each bough reminds of Yuletide cheer,
Of family, friends, and those held dear.
For garlands hung with thoughtful care,
Create a warmth beyond compare.
So deck your halls with garlands bright,
And feel their magic through the night.
For in their green, their scent, their glow,
The spirit of Christmas starts to grow.
And as the season comes and goes,
The garland's memory softly shows.
A symbol of the love we share,
A Christmas joy beyond compare.

36. The Christmas Carol

The carol rises, soft and clear,
A melody for all to hear.
It drifts through streets, through frosted air,
A song of love beyond compare.
Each verse a tale of holy birth,
Of peace descending to the earth.
The chorus swells, the voices blend,
A song of joy that knows no end.
The candles flicker, shadows play,
As carols chase the night away.
They fill the heart, they lift the soul,
And make the weary spirit whole.
From "Silent Night" to "Joyful King,"
The carols through the ages ring.
They bridge the past, they span the years,
And wash away all doubts and fears.
So join the song, let voices raise,
In timeless hymns of joy and praise.
For Christmas carols, pure and true,
Bring heaven's peace to me and you.
And when the singing fades to still,
Its echoes linger, warm and real.
For carols sung on Christmas Eve,
Leave love and hope for those who believe.

37. The Toymaker's Workshop

The toymaker works through frosty nights,
With tools that hum in gentle lights.
His hands create with steady care,
The gifts of dreams beyond compare.
The dolls, the trains, the teddy bears,
Each crafted with a heart that cares.
They wait for hands both small and sweet,
To bring their magic full complete.
The workshop hums, the elves all sing,
Of joy and love these toys will bring.
For every screw, each painted hue,
Holds Christmas magic, strong and true.
Though hidden from the world outside,
The toymaker works, his joy his guide.
He knows the smiles his toys will bring,
The laughter that will brightly ring.
And when the sleigh departs at last,
The toymaker smiles at work gone past.
For every gift that finds a home,
Carries the love from where it's grown.
So cherish every toy you hold,
Its story worth more than gold.
For in its frame, a dream does live,
A toymaker's heart, his gift to give.

38. The Christmas Eve Prayer

On Christmas Eve, we bow in prayer,
With hearts uplifted, spirits bare.
We give our thanks for love and light,
That grace our world on this pure night.
We pray for peace, for joy to grow,
For kindness shared with those we know.
And for the stranger, near and far,
We send our hope, a guiding star.
The candle burns, its flame so still,
A symbol of our hopeful will.
Its glow reflects in every eye,
A spark of faith that will not die.
Together, hands and hearts unite,
In gentle prayer this sacred night.
We ask for strength, for love's embrace,
To guide us through the year with grace.
And as the prayer begins to fade,
Its message in our souls is laid.
For Christmas Eve's most precious gift,
Is peace of heart and spirit's lift.
So let us pray, in quiet cheer,
For all we love, both far and near.
And may this prayer of hope and light,
Bring blessings on this Christmas night.

39. The Sleigh Bells' Song

The sleigh bells ring, a joyful sound,
Their jingle echoes all around.
They dance upon the frosty breeze,
A melody that brings us ease.
Their song is bright, their rhythm clear,
It sings of joy and Christmas cheer.
With every note, a smile appears,
A tune that lasts through all the years.
The bells accompany Santa's sleigh,
As reindeer glide along their way.
They mark the path through snowy skies,
A chorus where the magic lies.
The song they play, though short and sweet,
Is Christmas joy, a festive beat.
It calls to hearts both young and old,
A tale of warmth in winter's cold.
So when you hear their jingling tune,
Beneath the stars, beneath the moon,
Know that the bells, with every chime,
Bring Christmas love through space and time.
And as their echoes fade to still,
Their joy remains, a lasting thrill.
For sleigh bells sing in every heart,
A tune of love that won't depart.

40. The Snow Globe's World

A snow globe stands, so small, so bright,
Its world encased in crystal light.
With just a shake, the snowflakes fall,
A tiny scene that captures all.
Inside, a town of timeless cheer,
Where Christmas lives throughout the year.
The children play, the sleighs do glide,
As love and joy fill every side.
The snow swirls round in gentle dance,
A wonder held at just a glance.
It whispers softly, "Come and see,
The magic of eternity."
The globe reminds of simpler days,
Of carol songs and peaceful ways.
A perfect world in frosted glass,
Where every moment's meant to last.
So hold it close and watch it spin,
Let Christmas magic draw you in.
For in its glow, its quiet gleam,
You'll find the heart of every dream.
And when you set the globe to rest,
Its charm remains within your chest.
A snow globe's world, though small and still,
Holds Christmas love that warms and thrills.

41. The Gift of Friendship

A friend's kind heart, a friend's warm smile,
Can make life's journey worth the while.
Through Christmas joys, through winter's chill,
Their love and laughter guide us still.
A gift unwrapped, yet cherished true,
Is friendship shared by me and you.
It grows with time, it never fades,
A light that cuts through darkest shades.
Together round the fire's glow,
We share the tales of long ago.
We toast the times both good and bad,
And find the joy in all we've had.
For friends are gifts that time can't steal,
Their presence makes our hearts reveal,
The love that keeps us strong and whole,
The bond that lives within the soul.
So this Christmas, let's raise a cheer,
For friendships built year after year.
For in their love, we always find,
The truest gifts for heart and mind.
And though the seasons come and go,
This gift of friendship only grows.
A timeless treasure, bright and clear,
That warms our hearts through every year.

42. The Christmas Lantern

A lantern glows on Christmas night,
Its gentle flame a beacon bright.
It stands beside the frosted door,
A welcome sign to rich and poor.
Its light cuts through the winter's chill,
And casts a glow o'er field and hill.
It calls the weary traveler home,
No longer lost, no need to roam.
The lantern tells of hope's warm flame,
A light that burns in Christmas name.
It leads the way, it guides us near,
To hearts that hold the season dear.
Within its glass, the fire sways,
A silent hymn of love it plays.
It whispers softly, "All are one,"
Beneath the stars, beneath the sun.
So let your lantern shine with grace,
To brighten every weary face.
For in its glow, we all can see,
The love that binds both you and me.
And when the night gives way to day,
Its light will still show us the way.
A Christmas lantern, pure and true,
Illuminates the good we do.

43. The Christmas Bakery

The bakery hums with scents divine,
Of sugar, spice, and warm mulled wine.
The pastries rise, the cookies bake,
A sweet delight for all to take.
Each treat is made with careful hand,
A sprinkle here, a dusting grand.
From gingerbread to pies so sweet,
It's love that makes these works complete.
The windows fog with warmth inside,
As carolers sing and sleigh bells glide.
The baker smiles, with joy so clear,
For Christmas brings its magic near.
Each bite is more than taste alone,
It's memories and love well-known.
A simple treat can spark a flame,
Of joy and laughter, all the same.
So gather round the bakery's glow,
And let its wonders softly show.
For every pastry, cake, and pie,
Carries the warmth of Christmas sky.
And when the feast has reached its end,
The bakery's gifts still warmth extend.
For in its walls, the spirit stays,
A testament to festive days.

44. The Christmas Candle

The Christmas candle burns so bright,
It fills the room with peaceful light.
Its flicker dances, soft and slow,
A quiet warmth in winter's glow.
Its flame reflects on faces near,
Each gaze alight with Christmas cheer.
It tells a tale, both old and new,
Of love enduring, pure and true.
The candle stands through storm and gale,
A steadfast glow when spirits fail.
It shines its light through darkest nights,
A beacon of eternal sights.
Its wax may melt, its flame may fade,
But in its warmth, our hearts are made.
It teaches us through every year,
That love and hope will persevere.
So light a candle, let it shine,
And feel its peace in every line.
For Christmas lives in gentle rays,
That light the soul in quiet ways.
And though its flame may flicker low,
Its message stays, a steady glow.
The Christmas candle's lasting part,
Is found within each glowing heart.

45. The Gift of Forgiveness

A gentle word, a heartfelt plea,
Can set the burdened spirit free.
For Christmas brings the gift of grace,
To mend the wounds we all must face.
Forgiveness shines, a gift untold,
More precious than the purest gold.
It lifts the weight, it clears the air,
And shows the world how much we care.
The season calls for hearts to mend,
To turn a foe into a friend.
To let the past be washed away,
And start anew on Christmas Day.
For every heart that seeks repair,
Will find its peace in love and care.
The gift of mercy, freely given,
Restores the bonds once torn and riven.
So offer this, the greatest gift,
And feel your soul begin to lift.
For Christmas teaches, every year,
That love can conquer pain and fear.
And as the snow begins to fall,
Let forgiveness heal us all.
A gift of peace, a fresh new start,
To light the way for every heart.

46. The Holly and the Ivy

The holly bright, the ivy green,
Together weave a Christmas scene.
Their leaves entwined in endless cheer,
A symbol of the Yuletide year.
The holly boasts its berries red,
Like drops of joy where love is spread.
Its pointed leaves, though sharp and strong,
Protect the hearts where they belong.
The ivy climbs with graceful ease,
A touch of life through winter's freeze.
It wraps around the coldest tree,
And brings the hope of what will be.
Together, they adorn the halls,
Their beauty shines on every wall.
They whisper of the ancient lore,
Of Christmas love forevermore.
So let the holly, let the ivy,
Decorate your home so lively.
For in their greens, the truth is clear,
That life and love outlast the year.
And when the season fades away,
Their memory will gently stay.
A testament to love's embrace,
That grows in every time and place.

47. The Little Drummer Boy

With drum in hand, he makes his way,
To where the newborn Savior lay.
A humble child with gift so small,
Yet offers it with heart and all.
His drumbeat soft, a steady sound,
Resounds within the stable round.
It marks the love that fills the air,
A rhythm pure beyond compare.
The animals, in quiet awe,
Bear witness to the sight they saw.
A boy who gives with all his might,
His music shining through the night.
Though others bring their gifts of gold,
The drummer's gift, a tale retold.
For in his beat, a truth does lie,
That love is found in low and high.
So listen close on Christmas Eve,
To hear the beat for those who believe.
The little drummer still will play,
To honor Christ on Christmas Day.
And in his rhythm, hearts will find,
The joy of giving, pure and kind.
A timeless gift, a steady drum,
To welcome all, for love has come.

48. The Spirit of Christmas Giving

The spirit of giving fills the air,
A warmth that melts away despair.
It whispers softly, "Share your light,"
And turns the dark to shining bright.
From simple gifts to grand displays,
The love of giving lights our days.
A toy, a meal, a kind embrace,
Can brighten up the coldest place.
The act itself, though small it seems,
Can spark the joy of Christmas dreams.
For in each gift, a story grows,
Of love that only giving shows.
No treasure wrapped, no gold refined,
Compares to giving of the mind.
A thoughtful deed, a helping hand,
Is worth more than the finest strand.
So let this spirit guide us true,
In every little thing we do.
For Christmas giving, pure and bright,
Transforms the world with love's own light.
And as the season fades away,
Its spirit in our hearts will stay.
A timeless gift, a love to share,
That spreads its warmth through everywhere.

49. The Snowman's Promise

The snowman stands, so proud, so tall,
A cheerful sight for one and all.
His scarf of red, his hat askew,
He greets the world with frosty hue.
He promises, though cold winds blow,
To stand his ground through ice and snow.
A steadfast friend in winter's chill,
He watches o'er the silent hill.
Though children laugh and run away,
He keeps his post both night and day.
His coal eyes shine, his carrot nose,
A beacon bright when daylight goes.
But snowmen know their time is brief,
They melt away like autumn's leaf.
Yet in their hearts, a hope remains,
That joy will last through all terrains.
So when his form begins to fade,
Remember all the joy he made.
For snowmen, though they come and go,
Leave Christmas magic in their glow.
And when next winter's winds do call,
He'll rise again to greet us all.
A symbol of the joy and cheer,
That lives within the frosty year.

50. The Christmas Bell

The Christmas bell, with silver chime,
Rings out its song through wintertime.
Its echoes dance on frosty air,
And spread a message far and rare.
It tolls for peace, it tolls for joy,
For every girl and every boy.
Its voice proclaims the season's grace,
And fills with love each quiet space.
From steeples high to hearths below,
Its golden tones through homes will flow.
It calls the weary and the lost,
To find their peace, no matter cost.
The bell reminds of years gone by,
Of starry nights and snow-filled sky.
It sings of hope that never fades,
Through life's long journeys, all its shades.
So let its music fill your heart,
And play its role, a sacred part.
For in its chime, we hear anew,
The timeless gift of love so true.
And as the bell's last note does fade,
Its melody in hearts is laid.
A Christmas bell, with chime so clear,
Rings love and hope through every year.

51. The Gingerbread House

A gingerbread house, so sweetly made,
With candies bright and icing laid.
Its walls of spice, its roof of glaze,
Bring joy to all in festive days.
Each gumdrop placed with careful hand,
Each peppermint, a touch so grand.
The house becomes a sight to see,
A symbol of love's artistry.
The children gather, eyes aglow,
To marvel at the treats on show.
They build, they laugh, they decorate,
A memory time cannot abate.
The house may crumble, treats be gone,
But still its spirit lingers on.
For in its making, love was shown,
A gift of joy to call our own.
So bake your house with care and cheer,
And let its magic draw you near.
For gingerbread, with spice and sweet,
Makes Christmas moments pure and complete.
And when it's time to take a bite,
Remember all that made it right.
The joy of crafting, hand in hand,
A Christmas house that love has planned.

52. The Night Before Christmas

The world lies still on Christmas Eve,
A night of magic we believe.
The stars above, in silent glow,
Illuminate the earth below.
The children rest, their dreams take flight,
Of reindeer speeding through the night.
While stockings hung by fireside care,
Await the gifts soon to appear.
The clock strikes twelve, the sleigh bells ring,
A herald for the joy they bring.
And Santa smiles, his task begun,
To spread his cheer to everyone.
Through every home, through every town,
He brings the gifts and settles down.
A quiet laugh, a nod, a wink,
Then up he goes before we blink.
The morning comes, the joy is found,
With laughter ringing all around.
For Christmas magic, pure and bright,
Begins its work on this great night.
So let us cherish every cheer,
And hold its warmth throughout the year.
For Christmas Eve, with stars above,
Reminds us of a world in love.

53. The Christmas Choir

The choir gathers in the square,
Their voices lift in chilly air.
They sing of peace, of joy, of light,
And fill the town with pure delight.
Each note they sing, a gentle plea,
For love and hope in harmony.
Their carols echo far and wide,
A melody that hearts abide.
The crowd grows still, the song takes flight,
It wraps the world in softest light.
It calls for unity and cheer,
And holds the magic of the year.
From "Silent Night" to "Noel" sweet,
Their music makes the night complete.
It weaves a spell, it warms the soul,
It makes the weary spirit whole.
So let us join their festive tune,
Beneath the stars, beneath the moon.
For Christmas choirs, in voice so true,
Bring peace and love to me and you.
And as their final note is sung,
Its echoes linger, softly strung.
A choir's gift, both strong and clear,
Brings Christmas joy to all who hear.

54. The Fireplace Glow

The fireplace crackles, warm and bright,
A beacon in the frosty night.
Its flames reach high, they dance and play,
And keep the cold of winter at bay.
Around the hearth, we gather near,
To share in love and Christmas cheer.
With every spark, a story's told,
Of festive nights in days of old.
The fire hums a soothing tune,
It flickers soft beneath the moon.
Its golden glow on faces cast,
Creates a warmth that's sure to last.
The stockings hang in cheerful row,
Awaiting gifts from Santa's tow.
But more than gifts, this hearth does bring,
A bond of love in endless spring.
So let the fire's warmth embrace,
And light the love on every face.
For in its glow, we find anew,
The heart of Christmas shining through.
And when the embers start to fade,
The memories near the hearth are laid.
A Christmas fire, a timeless light,
To guide us through each winter night.

55. The Shepherd's Watch

The shepherds watch the quiet land,
With staff in grip, and lantern in hand.
The stars above, in silent glow,
Reveal the peace of fields below.
Then suddenly, a light so grand,
An angel's voice, a heaven-planned.
"Rejoice!" it calls, "A child is born,
To bring the light of Christmas morn."
With haste they travel, hearts alight,
To see the babe, a wondrous sight.
Within the manger, calm and still,
They find the hope of God's great will.
The sheep do bleat, the stars shine clear,
The shepherds know the Savior's near.
They kneel in awe, their spirits raised,
Their humble hearts in wonder dazed.
And from that night, their voices ring,
They share the joy the angels bring.
For shepherds, lowly though they be,
Were first to glimpse eternity.
So let us too, with hearts sincere,
Embrace the love that draws us near.
For in their watch, we come to see,
The joy of Christmas, pure and free.

56. The Christmas Tree's Secret

The Christmas tree, so tall and grand,
Was once a sapling in the land.
It grew with grace through sun and rain,
Its branches strong, its beauty plain.
But Christmas brought it to this place,
Where love and joy fill every space.
Adorned with lights and tinsel bright,
It stands a symbol in the night.
Each ornament a tale does tell,
Of years gone by, remembered well.
A child's first craft, a parent's care,
All hanging gently, memories rare.
The star above, it shines so true,
It points the way for me and you.
It crowns the tree with heavenly light,
A guide through every silent night.
And though the season soon will fade,
The tree's great secret is displayed:
That love, like leaves, will always grow,
Through every time, through ice and snow.
So let the Christmas tree remind,
Of all the joy we leave behind.
For every branch, each shining part,
Holds Christmas close within the heart.

57. The Christmas Parade

The Christmas parade winds through the street,
A festive march with drums and beat.
The floats pass by with lights aglow,
A moving show of holiday flow.
The marching bands, with songs so grand,
Fill hearts with cheer across the land.
Their melodies of joy and peace,
Make spirits rise, let worries cease.
The children wave, their eyes alight,
As dancers twirl in snow so white.
The reindeer prance, the elves all cheer,
For Santa's sleigh is drawing near.
Atop his sleigh, old Santa grins,
His bag of gifts, the joy begins.
He waves to all, both young and old,
And spreads the warmth of Christmas gold.
The parade, though brief, leaves hearts so full,
Its magic strong, its charm so pull.
For in its steps, we all can see,
The joy of Christmas unity.
And as it fades into the night,
Its echoes linger, pure delight.
A Christmas parade, both grand and true,
Brings holiday cheer to me and you.

58. The Warmth of Christmas Mittens

A pair of mittens, snug and warm,
Protects from every winter storm.
With woolen weave and patterned thread,
They guard against the frosty spread.
A child's small hands within them hide,
While snowballs form and sleighs do glide.
Their tiny palms stay safe from chill,
As winter plays on every hill.
Each mitten tells a story sweet,
Of love that wraps from head to feet.
A mother's care, a knitter's touch,
A gift of warmth that means so much.
Through snowball fights and frosty fun,
The mittens hold till day is done.
They gather snow but still they keep,
A cozy warmth through cold so deep.
So when you wear these mittens bright,
Remember those who brought their light.
For every stitch, both snug and tight,
Is love that warms on Christmas night.
And even when the winter's through,
Their warmth remains, a love so true.
A simple gift, yet grand in scope,
A pair of mittens, filled with hope.

59. The Yuletide Feast

The table set, a grand display,
A feast prepared for Christmas Day.
The roasted ham, the spiced mulled wine,
Invite us all to come and dine.
The family gathers, hand in hand,
Around the feast, so richly planned.
With every dish, a joy is shared,
With every toast, a love declared.
The laughter flows, the stories fly,
As plates are filled and spirits high.
Each bite a taste of festive cheer,
A memory made to last the year.
The pies and cakes, so sweetly laid,
Are treasures from the heart displayed.
They mark the love in every crumb,
And bring the warmth of Christmas home.
The feast is more than food and fare,
It's love and joy beyond compare.
A time to cherish, time to hold,
The bonds of family, pure as gold.
So let us raise a glass this night,
And toast to love in festive light.
For Christmas feasts, though soon they fade,
Leave hearts aglow, connections made.

60. The Magic of Christmas Morning

The dawn arrives, the light breaks through,
A world transformed by morning's hue.
The gifts are waiting, bright and bold,
As Christmas tales of joy unfold.
The children rush with shouts of glee,
To see what's placed beneath the tree.
Their laughter fills the morning air,
A harmony of love and care.
The paper tears, the ribbons fall,
Revealing treasures, large and small.
Yet more than toys, the morning brings,
A time to share life's simple things.
The hugs, the smiles, the joy that flows,
Is greater than what wrapping shows.
For Christmas morning softly weaves,
A magic only love achieves.
Together round the tree we stand,
A family joined, hand in hand.
The morning's light reveals anew,
The ties that bind, both strong and true.
And as the day unfolds its grace,
The morning's joy time won't erase.
For every heart holds Christmas near,
A morning full of love sincere.

61. The Midnight Snowfall

At midnight's stroke, the snow begins,
A quiet dance as time now spins.
The world transforms, a canvas white,
A gift from skies on Christmas night.
Each flake descends in gentle grace,
It blankets every street and place.
A hush envelops near and far,
Beneath the glow of one bright star.
The midnight snow, so soft, so pure,
Brings peace and calm that will endure.
It wraps the earth in tender care,
A silent prayer beyond compare.
The trees stand still in snowy gowns,
The rooftops wear their frosty crowns.
Each shimmering field, each shining hill,
Whispers of Christmas, calm and still.
So step outside, embrace the sight,
This wondrous gift of winter's night.
For midnight snow, though cold it seems,
Warms every heart with Christmas dreams.
And when the dawn begins to break,
The magic lingers in its wake.
For snow that falls on Christmas Eve,
Leaves beauty for those who believe.

62. The Gift of Hope

The gift of hope, so pure, so bright,
Illuminates the darkest night.
It lifts the heart, it clears the way,
And brings the dawn of Christmas Day.
In every heart, a spark resides,
A flame of hope that never hides.
It grows with love, it shines with cheer,
A beacon strong throughout the year.
Though trials come, though storms may roar,
This gift of hope will still endure.
It carries us through doubt and fear,
And brings us peace when skies are clear.
So let us share this gift divine,
A light that endlessly will shine.
For hope, once given, will take flight,
And fill the world with pure delight.
At Christmas time, let hope take hold,
A gift more precious than fine gold.
For in its glow, the soul can see,
The promise of what life can be.
And as the season comes to end,
Let hope remain, a faithful friend.
For every heart deserves to know,
The gift of hope, in endless glow.

63. The North Wind's Song

The north wind sings on Christmas Eve,
A haunting tune that we believe.
It whispers through the snowy trees,
A melody upon the breeze.
Its voice, though cold, is strangely warm,
It carries tales of love's great form.
It weaves a spell through frosted air,
And leaves its magic everywhere.
The wind recalls the shepherd's field,
The angel's song, the sky revealed.
It hums a hymn of peace and light,
Of miracles on holy night.
It moves the bells, it stirs the chimes,
It echoes through the Christmas times.
It calls to hearts, both far and near,
To gather close, to hold what's dear.
So when the north wind starts to sing,
Let every heart begin to cling.
For in its song, we come to know,
The love that makes the season glow.
And as it fades into the sky,
Its song remains, it won't say goodbye.
The north wind's tune, forever strong,
Is Christmas love, a timeless song.

64. The Nutcracker's Tale

The Nutcracker stands in grand array,
Awaiting dreams on Christmas Day.
With wooden grin and soldier's stance,
He guards the night in festive dance.
A girl once dreamed of lands afar,
Of sugar plums and shining stars.
She followed him through magic's door,
To places wondrous, tales of lore.
In candy lands where dreams take flight,
The Nutcracker led through the night.
He fought for love, he stood his ground,
And joy within her heart was found.
Though silent now, he still imparts,
A magic that can warm our hearts.
His tale reminds us, year by year,
That dreams and love are always near.
So place him high upon your shelf,
A storybook come to life itself.
For Nutcracker, with steadfast gaze,
Holds Christmas charm in countless ways.
And when the season fades once more,
His tale will rest in heart and lore.
A timeless guard through night and day,
The Nutcracker stands, come what may.

65. The Frosted Windowpane

The frosted windowpane does gleam,
A canvas for a winter's dream.
Its icy patterns, etched with care,
Reveal a world beyond compare.
The stars above, they softly glow,
Their light reflected on the snow.
Through frosty glass, the world appears,
A winter's tale of love and cheer.
The children press their hands and see,
A wonderland of snow and tree.
They draw with fingers, shapes and lines,
And fill the glass with festive signs.
The pane tells stories, old and new,
Of Christmas joys both bright and true.
Each snowflake, like a whispered prayer,
Adds magic to the chilly air.
So stand before this icy frame,
And see the world, never the same.
For frosted glass on Christmas night,
Transforms the dark with silvery light.
And when the sun begins to shine,
Its magic melts, but still, we find,
The frosted window's tale remains,
A memory on its crystal panes.

66. The Christmas Ornament

An ornament hangs upon the tree,
A tiny charm for all to see.
Its surface shines in candlelight,
A sparkling gem on Christmas night.
Each ornament a story tells,
Of family, friends, and Yuletide spells.
A child's small hand, a loved one's care,
Placed gently there with love to spare.
Some hold the past, their colors fade,
But in their age, sweet love is laid.
While others new, with vibrant gleam,
Bring future hopes and cherished dreams.
The tree becomes a living tale,
Of moments shared that never pale.
Each ornament a link to bind,
The love of hearts, both close and kind.
So as you trim your tree with care,
Remember all the love placed there.
For ornaments, though small they seem,
Hold Christmas joy in every beam.
And when the season fades away,
Their stories in your heart will stay.
A timeless bond, a cherished art,
The Christmas tree, love's beating heart.

67. The Christmas Pillow

A Christmas pillow, soft and bright,
Adds comfort on a winter night.
Its patterns stitched with festive thread,
Of snowflakes white and holly red.
It rests upon the couch or chair,
A place where love and rest repair.
Through laughter shared or quiet read,
It cradles every weary head.
Its softness speaks of peace and cheer,
A haven warm when cold draws near.
A simple touch, a gentle care,
That fills the home with love's sweet air.
The Christmas pillow tells no tale,
Yet comforts hearts when spirits fail.
It brings us close, it keeps us still,
A silent peace through winter's chill.
And when the season fades from view,
Its cozy warmth remains with you.
For in its softness, you will find,
A Christmas calm, both warm and kind.
So lay your head, let dreams take flight,
Upon this pillow Christmas night.
For love and peace will softly flow,
Through every stitch, through every snow.

68. The Yuletide Candlelight

The candle's flame, a golden hue,
Flickers softly, calm and true.
It lights the room in gentle glow,
And warms the heart through falling snow.
Its scent of pine or cinnamon sweet,
Fills every corner, every seat.
A beacon bright on winter's night,
A symbol of the season's light.
Its flame reflects on faces dear,
In quiet rooms or festive cheer.
It tells of peace, of love's embrace,
A steady glow in time and space.
Though winds may howl and snow may fall,
The candle's light will guide us all.
It whispers softly, "Do not fear,
For Christmas love is always near."
So light a candle, let it burn,
And feel the peace for which we yearn.
For in its glow, both small and grand,
The warmth of Christmas takes its stand.
And when its flame is gone from sight,
Its glow remains in hearts alight.
The Yuletide candle's gentle beam,
Is Christmas love's eternal dream.

69. The Winter's Garland

A garland made of winter's best,
Adorns the home, a welcome guest.
With evergreen and berries red,
It frames the doors where joy is spread.
Each needle points to life anew,
Though snow may fall, its strength is true.
It drapes the halls, it crowns the hearth,
A symbol of the season's worth.
The garland whispers tales of old,
Of snowy nights and fireside gold.
It weaves together love and cheer,
And draws us close, both far and near.
With ribbon twined and candles bright,
It brings the warmth of festive light.
A simple strand, yet bold and strong,
It carries Christmas all along.
So hang it high with tender care,
Let winter's garland grace the air.
For in its green, its scent, its charm,
We find a love both pure and warm.
And when the season comes to close,
The garland's memory softly shows.
A timeless piece of Christmas lore,
That lives within forevermore.

70. The Joy of Wrapping Gifts

With ribbons curled and paper bright,
We wrap the gifts on Christmas night.
Each fold and bow, with care applied,
A love that's wrapped and set aside.
The paper crinkles, scissors glide,
As hidden treasures wait inside.
Each gift a token, simple, small,
Yet holds the joy of giving all.
The tape is pressed, the tag is tied,
A heartfelt message placed with pride.
For in these parcels, love resides,
A cherished bond that never hides.
The joy of wrapping's more than art,
It's crafting love from heart to heart.
A secret shared, a thoughtful deed,
That fills the world with what we need.
And when they're opened, piece by piece,
The joy of giving will not cease.
For every ribbon, torn and tossed,
Reflects a love that's never lost.
So wrap with care, and let it show,
The thought and warmth you long to grow.
For Christmas gifts, though wrapped with skill,
Hold love that lingers, lasting still.

71. The Holly Crown

A crown of holly, green and red,
Adorns the table, neatly spread.
Its berries bright, its leaves so bold,
A festive sight from tales of old.
It circles round with endless grace,
A timeless touch in every place.
Its thorns remind of trials past,
Yet love and joy will always last.
The holly crown, both sharp and sweet,
Brings balance to the Yuletide feat.
It tells of life through winter's chill,
A stubborn love that warms us still.
Placed on the mantel or the door,
It welcomes all who venture o'er.
A sign of peace, a pledge to care,
That Christmas spirit's everywhere.
And when the season bids adieu,
The holly crown remains with you.
Its memory speaks of love profound,
A Christmas gift, forever bound.

72. The Gift of a Hug

A hug, so simple, yet so dear,
Can fill the heart with Christmas cheer.
No need for bows or tags to tie,
It's love that's shared with you and I.
Its warmth can melt the coldest chill,
It soothes the soul, it bends the will.
It speaks of comfort, calm, and peace,
And lets the heartache find release.
A hug can say what words cannot,
It holds the space where love is wrought.
A gift that costs no coin or gold,
Yet in its arms, great wealth is told.
So give this gift with open arms,
Let Christmas weave its healing charms.
For every hug, both strong and true,
Carries the love that binds us through.
And when the season comes to close,
This gift of hugs, its power shows.
For in its grasp, we come to see,
The heart of Christmas unity.

73. The Mistletoe's Kiss

Beneath the mistletoe's green embrace,
Two hearts find love in a quiet place.
Its berries white, its leaves so fine,
A symbol of joy in festive time.
A gentle kiss, a moment shared,
A bond of love, both strong and rare.
The mistletoe, though small it seems,
Creates a world of cherished dreams.
It hangs above in secret glee,
A silent call for you and me.
To pause and share a loving smile,
And make this season all worthwhile.
For mistletoe's magic, soft and sweet,
Brings hearts together where they meet.
Its charm invites both love and cheer,
To fill the world this time of year.
And when the mistletoe is gone,
Its memory of love lives on.
A timeless gift, a whispered bliss,
That starts beneath a Christmas kiss.

74. The Christmas Clock

The Christmas clock ticks soft and slow,
Its steady rhythm marks the glow.
Of moments shared, of time well-spent,
Of love and peace, this season's scent.
Its hands move gently, hour by hour,
Through festive nights and morning's power.
It chimes at last on Christmas Day,
A herald of joy in its own way.
The clock reminds of time so fleet,
Of memories made and hearts that meet.
For every second, small or grand,
Carries the touch of love's sweet hand.
The past and future, both entwined,
Are held within its ticking mind.
It whispers softly, "Cherish now,
For time is fleeting; make your vow."
So as the Christmas clock does chime,
Embrace the present, mark the time.
For moments spent with those you hold,
Are treasures worth more than pure gold.
And when the season fades away,
The Christmas clock, though quiet, stays.
A constant guide, a faithful friend,
That marks the time where love won't end.

75. The Carol of the Bells

The bells begin their lilting song,
A carol bright that rings along.
They echo through the chilly night,
A call for joy, a pure delight.
Their tones cascade in rhythmic cheer,
A harmony for all to hear.
They dance upon the frosty air,
A melody beyond compare.
The carol tells of love's great light,
Of peace descending on this night.
It weaves a tale of hope and grace,
That warms the coldest, darkest place.
From steeples high to streets below,
Their music sets the world aglow.
It lifts the weary, soothes the soul,
And makes the broken spirit whole.
So let the carol ring out clear,
And fill the world with Christmas cheer.
For in its notes, the heart will find,
A joy that's lasting, pure, and kind.
And when the bells have sung their part,
Their echoes linger in the heart.
A carol bright that never ends,
A song of love that time defends.

76. The Silent Forest

The forest stands in quiet grace,
A tranquil, snowy, sacred place.
Its branches bare, its leaves all gone,
Yet Christmas light still lingers on.
The pines rise high, their needles green,
A living symbol of serene.
Their boughs hold snow, like gentle hands,
Protecting all of winter's lands.
The silence speaks in hushed, soft tones,
A peaceful calm the forest owns.
It tells of life beneath the frost,
Of hidden beauty never lost.
The animals tread with careful steps,
Through snowy paths their journey's kept.
And in their eyes, a quiet cheer,
For Christmas brings its peace so near.
So wander through this forest still,
And feel its love, its quiet thrill.
For in its calm, you'll come to see,
The heart of Christmas, wild and free.
And when you leave its tranquil space,
The forest's peace will still embrace.
A gift of calm, a quiet song,
To carry in your heart lifelong.

77. The Christmas Scarf

A scarf of wool, both soft and warm,
Protects against the winter storm.
Its colors bright, its fabric fine,
A gift of love through snowy time.
It wraps around with gentle care,
To shield from cold, from frosty air.
Its length provides a snug embrace,
A portable warmth, a soft, safe space.
Each stitch a sign of love's own thread,
Of thoughts and prayers in colors spread.
A scarf may seem so small, so light,
Yet holds the power of Christmas night.
Through icy winds and blustery gales,
It tells a tale that never fails.
Of care extended, freely shown,
A warmth that makes the heart feel known.
So wear this scarf with joy and pride,
Let Christmas love in you abide.
For in its threads, you'll always find,
A bond that warms both heart and mind.
And even when the chill has passed,
Its memory will always last.
A simple gift, but oh, so grand,
A Christmas scarf, by loving hand.

78. The Angel's Song

High above, the angels sing,
A song of peace their voices bring.
Their harmonies fill winter's night,
A chorus bathed in holy light.
Their song descends on wings of grace,
It touches every time and place.
A melody of love and cheer,
That softly whispers, "God is near."
The shepherds hear, their hearts take flight,
They leave their flocks to seek the sight.
For in the song, they find their way,
To where the Savior child does lay.
The angels sing of hope's rebirth,
Of lasting peace upon the earth.
Their voices lift, both strong and true,
A hymn of love for me and you.
So listen close on Christmas Eve,
And let their song help you believe.
For angel choirs still softly call,
A timeless love that reaches all.
And when the dawn breaks on the morn,
Their song remains, forever sworn.
A Christmas hymn, both deep and strong,
The angels' everlasting song.

79. The Christmas Star's Journey

The Christmas star begins its climb,
Through quiet skies in ancient time.
It shines its light, a path to show,
For those who seek the love below.
Its golden rays, both pure and bright,
Guide travelers through the silent night.
The wise men follow, hearts aglow,
With treasures for the child they know.
Above the stable, soft and clear,
The star proclaims, "The Lord is near."
Its glow brings peace to all who see,
A light for all eternity.
No matter where the journey leads,
The star provides for every need.
It whispers hope, it points the way,
To love that dawns on Christmas Day.
So look above, and find its gleam,
A light of joy, a guiding beam.
For in its glow, we too can share,
The Christmas hope that's always there.
And as the years go swiftly by,
The Christmas star remains on high.
A symbol of the love we hold,
A story of wonder, forever told.

80. The Christmas Cabin

A cabin stands in snowy wood,
Its chimney puffs, as warm it should.
The fire inside, with glowing light,
Keeps winter's chill from creeping tight.
The logs are stacked, the blankets spread,
The family gathers, joy ahead.
They tell their tales, they share their cheer,
As Christmas Eve draws ever near.
The cabin hums with life and song,
A refuge when the nights are long.
Its walls embrace the love within,
A sacred place where dreams begin.
Outside, the snow falls soft and deep,
While those inside are fast asleep.
They dream of gifts and morning's glow,
Of all the joys the season shows.
The Christmas cabin, strong and true,
Stands firm through storms and skies of blue.
A home where love will always reign,
Through every joy, through every pain.
And when the dawn breaks crisp and clear,
The cabin wakes with Christmas near.
Its warmth and light, its love and song,
Will hold us close, our whole life long.

81. The Sleigh Bells' Journey

The sleigh bells jingle, crisp and bright,
They cut through silent winter night.
With every ring, a joy they bring,
A sound of hope on frosty wing.
From village lanes to mountain tall,
Their echoes dance, they gently call.
They mark the path of Santa's flight,
A trail of love in soft moonlight.
The children hear and smile in bed,
Their dreams of toys swirl in their head.
Each chime a promise, strong and true,
That magic lives for me and you.
The sleigh bells' song, though sweet and brief,
Can melt away the heart's old grief.
It wraps the world in festive cheer,
And fills the soul with peace sincere.
So when you hear their distant sound,
Let Christmas joy in you abound.
For slcigh bells tell, in every chime,
The tale of love through endless time.
And as they fade into the night,
Their echoes linger, pure and light.
The sleigh bells' journey never ends,
A song of love that time defends.

82. The Christmas Market's Glow

The market hums with festive cheer,
As Christmas draws its magic near.
The stalls are filled with treats and toys,
With treasures bright for girls and boys.
The air is rich with scents of spice,
Of roasted nuts and warm mince pies.
The chatter hums, the laughter flies,
As joy and wonder light the skies.
The vendors smile with friendly call,
Their wares displayed for one and all.
Each bauble shines, each trinket gleams,
A perfect piece for Christmas dreams.
The carolers sing in gentle tune,
Beneath the stars and silver moon.
Their voices lift in harmony,
A song of peace for all to see.
So wander through this festive place,
And see the joy on every face.
For Christmas markets, small or grand,
Bring love and cheer to every land.
And when the market lights grow dim,
Its spirit sings a lasting hymn.
A memory bright, a cherished show,
The magic of the market's glow.

83. The Silent Night's Embrace

The silent night wraps all in peace,
Its calm provides a sweet release.
The world slows down, the stars align,
And whispers tell of love divine.
The trees stand still in snowy white,
Beneath the glow of soft moonlight.
The world, though cold, feels warm and near,
As Christmas magic draws us near.
Each breath we take, both calm and deep,
Is wrapped in stillness, soft as sleep.
The silent night, so full of grace,
Provides a sacred, quiet space.
It holds the dreams of those who pray,
For brighter dawns and peaceful days.
Its quiet hum, though soft, is strong,
It soothes the heart, it rights the wrong.
So when the night is calm and clear,
Embrace its peace, let love draw near.
For in the stillness, hearts will see,
The gift of Christmas purity.
And as the morning light appears,
Its quiet peace will dry our tears.
The silent night, a gentle thread,
That weaves its love through all we've said.

84. The Christmas Eve Hearth

The hearth burns bright on Christmas Eve,
Its flicker gives more than you'd believe.
It tells of warmth, it speaks of cheer,
A gathering place for those held dear.
The flames leap high, they softly sing,
Of peace and love the season brings.
Their golden light on faces play,
A warm embrace at end of day.
The family sits, with hands entwined,
A scene of love, a joy defined.
They share their stories, dreams unfold,
As firelight weaves a tale of old.
The hearth becomes a sacred place,
Where hearts are warmed, and time slows pace.
It whispers truths we hold so dear,
That Christmas love will conquer fear.
And though the night may fade away,
Its glow remains through Christmas Day.
A hearth of light, a hearth of song,
That keeps us safe our whole life long.
So gather close, and let it show,
The love that only Christmas knows.
For in its warmth, both bold and sweet,
The heart of Christmas finds its beat.

85. The Christmas Eve Lantern

A lantern glows on Christmas Eve,
Its gentle light helps hearts believe.
It casts a path through snow and pine,
A guiding flame, a sign divine.
Its glass reflects the starry skies,
As wonder dances in our eyes.
It leads us home through frosty air,
To find the love that waits us there.
The lantern hums a quiet song,
Of hope and peace where we belong.
Its steady light, both strong and true,
Illuminates the world anew.
Through every storm, through wind and snow,
The lantern's glow will always show.
A beacon for the lost and stray,
It lights the path on Christmas Day.
So let it shine, both near and far,
A humble light, a steadfast star.
For in its flame, we come to see,
The warmth of love and unity.
And when the night turns into morn,
The lantern's light will not be worn.
It stays within, a spark of grace,
To guide us through life's every space.

86. The Christmas Choir's Echo

The Christmas choir lifts its song,
A melody both clear and strong.
It soars above, it fills the night,
With harmonies of pure delight.
Each note, a call to every heart,
A gentle pull, a loving start.
It speaks of peace, it sings of grace,
It carries joy to every place.
The voices blend in perfect tune,
Beneath the stars, beneath the moon.
They rise and fall like waves at sea,
A Christmas hymn of unity.
The crowd stands still, their spirits high,
As music echoes through the sky.
It warms the soul, it lifts the mind,
And leaves the troubles far behind.
So let the choir's song endure,
A timeless gift, a joy so pure.
For every note, both high and low,
Brings Christmas love where'er we go.
And even when their song is done,
Its echoes linger, one by one.
A symphony of hope and cheer,
That stays within throughout the year.

87. The Reindeer's Secret

The reindeer know the secret flight,
That takes them through the starry night.
They glide on winds both swift and strong,
To carry Santa's sleigh along.
Through snowy peaks and valleys low,
Their hooves leave tracks in moonlit snow.
They journey far, they journey wide,
With Christmas cheer as their true guide.
Each reindeer holds a special role,
A bond that makes the journey whole.
With every leap, with every run,
They bring the light of Christmas fun.
Though silent in their midnight quest,
Their hearts beat strong within each chest.
For they believe, and so they fly,
To spread the magic through the sky.
And when the morning light appears,
Their secret fades, but love adheres.
For reindeer, though they take their leave,
Leave Christmas joy on which we believe.
So listen close on Christmas Eve,
For sounds of hooves, and just believe.
For in their flight, the world does find,
A Christmas truth both bold and kind.

88. The Gift of a Song

A song, a gift from heart to heart,
Can brighten nights, a love impart.
Its melody, both soft and clear,
Brings warmth and joy to all who hear.
It needs no wrapping, needs no bow,
Yet in its notes, the love will show.
For every tune, both bright and sweet,
Carries a gift that's pure, complete.
A carol sung by fire's glow,
Brings peace and calm like falling snow.
It tells of hope, it tells of light,
A timeless joy on Christmas night.
So sing aloud, let voices raise,
And fill the world with songs of praise.
For music's gift, both small and grand,
Unites us all, hand in hand.
And even when the song is done,
Its harmony lives on as one.
A Christmas gift, so freely shared,
A love that lingers, deeply cared.
So let your song take flight this year,
A melody for all to hear.
For in its tune, the world will see,
The gift of love in harmony.

89. The Snowflake's Tale

A snowflake falls from skies above,
A tiny work of art and love.
Its journey long, its path unknown,
To rest upon the earth alone.
Each flake unique, a tale to tell,
Of winter's charm and Christmas spell.
It drifts through air with gentle glide,
A fleeting beauty far and wide.
It lands on rooftops, trees, and ground,
And softly blankets all around.
Together, flakes create a scene,
Of glistening white and peaceful sheen.
Though snow may melt as seasons pass,
Its memory stays like frosted glass.
For every flake, both small and slight,
Carries the magic of Christmas night.
So when you see them floating down,
Remember their celestial crown.
For snowflakes tell, in whispered lore,
Of love and joy forevermore.
And though their time on earth is brief,
They fill our hearts with sweet relief.
A gift from heaven, pure and true,
The snowflake's tale is meant for you.

90. The Christmas Pie

The Christmas pie, a treat so fine,
Adorned with crust and fruit divine.
Its golden top, its sugared glow,
A festive warmth through cold and snow.
With every slice, a flavor bright,
It brings delight on Christmas night.
The spices mix, the fruits combine,
To craft a taste both sweet and fine.
The table hums with laughter's sound,
As pie is passed and joy abounds.
Each forkful taken, slow and sure,
Is love and cheer, a taste so pure.
The pie, though simple, holds a key,
To Christmas love and unity.
It gathers hearts, it draws us near,
To share in joy, to spread good cheer.
And when the last slice disappears,
Its memory lingers through the years.
For Christmas pie, with warmth and glee,
Fills more than plates—it fills family.
So bake your pie with love and care,
And let its magic fill the air.
For in its sweetness, you will find,
A Christmas spirit, warm and kind.

91. The Tinsel's Dance

The tinsel shimmers in the light,
It sways and sparkles, pure delight.
Draped gently on the Christmas tree,
It dances bright for all to see.
Each strand reflects the candle's glow,
A silver ribbon, soft and slow.
It whispers tales of winter's charm,
And wraps the home in festive calm.
The tinsel knows the season's grace,
It weaves its joy through every space.
A simple touch, a glistening thread,
Transforms the tree with light it spreads.
Its beauty lies in how it shares,
A little magic, unaware.
For even in its silent dance,
It gives the world a second glance.
So let it hang, let tinsel play,
And watch it twinkle, night to day.
For in its strands, both light and sweet,
The heart of Christmas finds its beat.
And when the season fades from view,
The tinsel's memory stays with you.
A sparkling joy, a gentle trance,
The timeless charm of tinsel's dance.

92. The Christmas Tree Farm

Among the rows of pines so tall,
The Christmas trees await their call.
They stand in snow, both young and old,
Their branches strong, their stories told.
A family walks through frosty air,
To find the tree beyond compare.
They laugh, they search, their spirits high,
Beneath the wide and starry sky.
Each tree, a symbol of the cheer,
That lights the world this time of year.
With careful hands, they choose the one,
Their Christmas journey just begun.
The saw bites through, the tree falls low,
It's carried home through fields of snow.
To stand adorned with lights and love,
A festive gift from earth above.
The farm now waits, its trees still stand,
Awaiting joy throughout the land.
For every tree that finds a place,
Brings Christmas cheer and warm embrace.
And when the season comes to close,
The farm will sleep beneath the snows.
But every tree, in every home,
Carries the magic, love has sown.

93. The Christmas Sleigh

The sleigh stands ready in the yard,
Its runners gleam, its paint unmarred.
The reins are strong, the horses bright,
Prepared to ride through winter's night.
The family climbs, their spirits soar,
As bells begin their joyful score.
Through snowy fields, the sleigh does glide,
With love and laughter side by side.
The stars above, the frosty breeze,
Enhance the joy of nights like these.
Each jingle rings with festive cheer,
A harmony of hearts held near.
The horses trot, their pace is sure,
Through winding paths and forests pure.
The sleigh ride, though a simple joy,
Brings lasting memories to employ.
And as they reach their journey's end,
They smile and laugh with hearts to mend.
For in the sleigh, through cold and play,
They found the love of Christmas Day.
So let the sleigh's old runners glide,
Through snowy trails both far and wide.
For every journey that it takes,
A lasting Christmas joy it makes.

94. The Christmas Stocking's Tale

The stocking hung with tender care,
Awaits its gifts, a promise rare.
Its fabric holds a silent plea,
For love and joy beneath the tree.
Each stitch, a mark of years gone by,
Of Christmas mornings flying high.
It stands as proof of hearts made light,
Of dreams fulfilled on winter's night.
The small surprises tucked inside,
Are tokens of the love we hide.
A candy cane, a tiny toy,
A secret shared, a spark of joy.
The stocking's tale is one of grace,
It brings a smile to every face.
For though its treasures may be small,
Its meaning towers over all.
And as it sways by fire's glow,
Its warmth and magic surely grow.
The stocking holds, through age and time,
A legacy of love sublime.
So hang it high, and let it tell,
Of Christmas joys that always swell.
For every stocking, plain or grand,
Holds Christmas love in every strand.

95. The First Snowfall of Christmas

The first snow falls on Christmas Eve,
A gift the skies let hearts receive.
Its flakes drift down, so pure, so light,
They cloak the world in gentle white.
The rooftops gleam, the branches glow,
The earth adorned in peaceful snow.
A quiet calm descends on all,
As Christmas magic answers call.
The children press against the pane,
To watch the snowflakes softly rain.
Their laughter bright, their spirits free,
They dream of wonders yet to be.
The first snowfall, a sacred sign,
Of love's renewal, pure, divine.
It blankets all in winter's peace,
A moment where our hearts find ease.
So step outside, let snowflakes fall,
And hear the whispers in their call.
For Christmas snow, both soft and deep,
Leaves love and joy for us to keep.
And as the morning light breaks through,
Its beauty stays, forever new.
The first snowfall of Christmas cheer,
Marks love and hope throughout the year.

96. The Joy of Giving

The joy of giving fills the air,
A love that shows we truly care.
A simple act, a thoughtful deed,
Can touch a heart in deepest need.
A wrapped-up gift, a helping hand,
Can spread the warmth through every land.
No matter small, no matter grand,
Its joy will linger where it stands.
The giver finds a special light,
That fills their soul on Christmas night.
For giving freely, hearts expand,
A treasure greater than the planned.
The joy of giving doesn't end,
It grows and spreads, it will transcend.
Through every gift, both near and far,
We light the world like Christmas stars.
So give with love, and let it show,
The peace and joy that hearts bestow.
For in this act, we all will see,
The true spirit of Christmas, free.
And long beyond the season's glow,
The joy of giving will still flow.
A gift of love, a gift of cheer,
That lives within us every year.

97. The Joy of Christmas Baking

The kitchen hums with festive cheer,
As Christmas baking draws us near.
The flour flies, the spices blend,
A sweet tradition without end.
The rolling pin moves to and fro,
As dough takes shape in even rows.
From gingerbread to sugar treats,
The air is filled with scents so sweet.
The cookies bake, their edges gold,
Each one a story gently told.
Of hands that knead and hearts that care,
Of love that fills the frosty air.
The children laugh, the oven glows,
The joy of baking softly shows.
For every treat, both small and grand,
Is crafted with a loving hand.
And when the trays are set to cool,
The kitchen feels like Christmas school.
A place where joy and love combine,
In every crumb, in every line.
So bake your treats and let them share,
The warmth and love beyond compare.
For Christmas baking, sweet and true,
Brings joy to all, both old and new.

98. The Christmas Postcard

A postcard sent from far away,
Brings Christmas cheer to brighten day.
Its picture shows a winter scene,
Of snowy trees and skies serene.
The message written, short and sweet,
Conveys a love no time can beat.
It bridges miles, it spans the sea,
To bring us close, both you and me.
The words within, though few they seem,
Can light the heart like Christmas dream.
For in each line, a love does grow,
A bond that only Christmas knows.
The postcard rests on mantel high,
A cherished sight beneath the sky.
It stands as proof that love transcends,
And reaches far to all our friends.
So write your cards with thoughtful care,
And let your heart in them declare.
For Christmas postcards, near or far,
Are letters sent from love's own star.
And as the seasons come and go,
Their words of joy will always show.
A timeless gift, a heartfelt start,
A Christmas treasure for the heart.

99. The Warm Glow of Christmas Lights

The Christmas lights, a radiant show,
Illuminate the world below.
Their colors dance on frosty nights,
Transforming homes with twinkling sights.
They line the rooftops, wrap the trees,
They sparkle softly in the breeze.
A simple string, yet grand they seem,
They turn the world to Christmas dream.
Each bulb a beacon, small but bright,
Reminding us of love's pure light.
Together shining, bold and clear,
They guide us through the festive year.
The lights reflect in eyes so wide,
As children watch them side by side.
Their glow inspires, their warmth reveals,
A joy that every heart soon feels.
So let the Christmas lights remain,
To chase away the dark and pain.
For in their glow, we find our way,
To peace and love on Christmas Day.
And even when the season ends,
Their memory through time extends.
A constant glow, a steadfast might,
The lasting charm of Christmas light.

100. The Spirit of Christmas Day

The dawn arrives on Christmas Day,
A world of joy on full display.
The morning hums with festive cheer,
A sacred time, both calm and clear.
The gifts are opened, laughter rings,
The family gathers, each heart sings.
The love exchanged in simple ways,
Fills every corner, every phrase.
The day unfolds with gentle grace,
As warmth and kindness find their place.
A meal is shared, a story told,
A treasure worth far more than gold.
For Christmas Day, beyond the tree,
Reminds us of our unity.
It's in the hugs, the songs, the light,
That Christmas spirit takes its flight.
And as the evening settles near,
We hold its magic close and dear.
For though the day may fade from sight,
Its love endures through every night.
So cherish this, the Christmas way,
The peace and joy of Christmas Day.
For in its heart, we always find,
A gift of love for all mankind.